MODESTY, MAKEOVERS,

and the Pursuit of Physical

BEAUTY

What Mothers and Daughters Need to Know

JEFFREY R. HOLLAND
AND SUSAN W. TANNER

DESERET
BOOK

SALT LAKE CITY, UTAH

"To Mothers and Daughters" by Elder Jeffrey R. Holland was originally published as "To Young Women" in *Ensign,* November 2005, 28–30.

"The Sanctity of the Body" by Susan W. Tanner was originally published in *Ensign,* November 2005, 13–15.

Photographs on pages 8–9, 24, 41, and 50–51 © Don Busath Photography. Used by permission.

Library of Congress Cataloging-in-Publication Data

Holland, Jeffrey R., 1940-
 Modesty, makeovers, and the pursuit of physical beauty : what mothers and daughters need to know / Jeffrey R. Holland, Susan W. Tanner.
  p.   cm.
 ISBN 1-59038-603-5 (hardcover : alk. paper)
 1. Modesty—Religious aspects—Christianity.   2. Body, Human—Religious aspects—Christianity.   3. Beauty, Personal.   4. Self-perception—Religious aspects—Christianity.   5. Church of Jesus Christ of Latter-day Saints—Doctrines.   6. Mormon Church—Doctrines.   I. Tanner, Susan W.   II. Title.
  BV4647.M63H65 2006
  248.8′33088289332—dc22   2006003961

Printed in the United States of America
Publishers Printing, Salt Lake City, Utah
10   9   8   7   6   5   4   3   2   1

CONTENTS

To Mothers and Daughters

Jeffrey R. Holland

Father Time played a rude trick on me just a few months ago. I arose one morning all bright eyed and bushy tailed, greeted the dawn with a smile—only to realize suddenly that with the birthday to be celebrated that day I now had a teenage grandchild. I thought about it for a minute and then did what any responsible, dignified adult would do. I got back in bed and pulled the covers over my head.

Traditional joking aside about the harrowing experience of raising teenagers, I want my own granddaughter and the vast majority of the youth of the Church whom I meet around the world to know how extraordinarily proud we are of you. Moral and physical danger exist almost everywhere around you and temptations of a dozen kinds present themselves daily, yet most of you strive to do what is right.

I wish to share my praise of you, to express my love, my encouragement, and my admiration for you. Because this precious eldest grandchild of mine is a young woman, I am going to address my remarks to the young women of the Church, but I hope the spirit of my message can apply to women and men of all ages. However, as Maurice Chevalier used to sing, I want to "thank heaven for little girls."

First of all, I want you to be proud you are a woman. I want you to feel the reality of what that means, to know who you truly are. You are literally a spirit daughter of heavenly parents with a divine nature and an eternal destiny.[1] That surpassing truth should be fixed deep in your soul and be

fundamental to every decision you make as you grow into mature womanhood. There could never be a greater authentication of your dignity, your worth, your privileges, and your promise. Your Father in Heaven knows your name and knows your circumstance. He hears your prayers. He knows your hopes and dreams, including your fears and frustrations. And He knows what you can become through faith in Him. Because of this divine heritage you, along with all of your spiritual sisters and brothers, have full equality in His sight and are empowered through obedience to become a rightful heir in His eternal kingdom, an "[heir] of God, and joint-[heir] with Christ" (Romans 8:17). Seek to comprehend the significance of these doctrines. Everything Christ taught He taught to women as well as men. Indeed, in the restored light of the gospel of Jesus Christ, a woman, including a young woman, occupies a majesty all her own in the divine design of the

Your Father in Heaven knows your name and knows your circumstance. And He knows what you can become through faith in Him.

Creator. You are, as Elder James E. Talmage once phrased it, "a sanctified investiture which none shall dare profane."[2]

Be a woman of Christ. Cherish your esteemed place in the sight of God. He needs you. This Church needs you. The world needs you. A woman's abiding trust in God and unfailing devotion to things of the Spirit have always been an anchor when the wind and the waves of life were fiercest.[3]

I say to you what the Prophet Joseph said more than 150 years ago: "If you live up to your privileges, the angels cannot be restrained from being your associates."[4]

All of this is to try to tell you how your Father in Heaven feels about you and what He has designed for you to become. And if for a time any of you are less visionary than this or seem bent on living beneath your privilege, then we express even greater love for you and plead with you to make your teenage years a triumph, not a tragedy. Fathers and mothers, prophets and apostles have no motive except to bless your life and to spare you every possible heartache.

For you to fully claim Heavenly Father's blessings and protection, we ask you to stay true to the standards of the gospel of Jesus Christ and *not* slavishly follow the whims of fads and fashions. The Church will never deny your moral agency regarding what you should wear and exactly how you should look. But the Church will always declare standards and will always teach principles. One of those principles is modesty. In the gospel of Jesus Christ, modesty in appearance is *always* in fashion. Our standards are *not* socially negotiable.

The *For the Strength of Youth* pamphlet is very clear in its call for young women to avoid clothing that is too tight, too short, or improperly revealing in any manner, including bare midriffs.[5] Parents, please review this booklet with your children. Second only to your love, they need your limits. Young women, choose your clothing the way you would choose your friends—in both cases choose that which improves you and would give you confidence standing in the presence of God (see D&C 121:45). Good friends would never embarrass you, demean you, or exploit you. Neither should your clothing.

I make a special appeal regarding how young women might dress for Church services and Sabbath worship. We used to speak of "best dress" or "Sunday dress," and maybe we should do so again. In any case, from ancient times to modern we have always been invited to present our best selves inside and out when entering the house of the Lord—and a dedicated LDS chapel is a "house of the Lord." Our clothing or footwear need never be expensive, indeed should *not* be expensive, but neither should it appear that we are on our way to the beach. When

BE A WOMAN OF CHRIST.

CHERISH YOUR ESTEEMED

PLACE IN THE SIGHT OF GOD.

HE NEEDS YOU.

we come to worship the God and Father of us all and to partake of the sacrament symbolizing the Atonement of Jesus Christ, we should be as comely and respectful, as dignified and appropriate as we can be. We should be recognizable in appearance as well as in behavior that we truly are disciples of Christ, that in a spirit of worship we are meek and lowly of heart, that we truly desire the Savior's Spirit to be with us always.

In this same vein may I address an even more sensitive subject. I plead with you young women to please be more accepting of yourselves, including your body shape and style, with a little less longing to look like someone else. We are all different. Some are tall, and some are short. Some are round, and some are thin. And almost everyone at some time or other wants to be something they are not! But as one adviser to teenage girls said: "You can't live your life worrying that the world is staring at you. When you let people's opinions make you self-conscious you give away your power. . . . The key to feeling [confident] is to always listen to your inner self—[the *real* you.]"[6] And in the kingdom of God, the real you is "more precious than rubies" (Proverbs 3:15). Every young woman is a child of destiny and every adult woman a powerful force for good. I mention adult women because, sisters, you are our greatest examples and resource for these young women. And if you are obsessing over being a size 2, you won't be very surprised when your daughter or the Mia Maid in your class does the same and makes herself physically ill trying to accomplish it. We should all be as fit as we can be—that's good Word of Wisdom doctrine. That means eating right and exercising and helping our bodies function at their optimum strength. We could probably all do better in that regard. But I speak here of optimum health; there is no universal optimum size.

Frankly, the world has been brutal with you in this regard. You are bombarded in movies, television, fashion magazines, and advertisements with the message that looks are everything! The pitch is, "If your looks are good enough, your life will be glamorous and you will be happy and popular." That kind of pressure is immense in the teenage years, to say nothing of later womanhood. In too many cases too much is being done to the human body to meet just such a fictional (to say nothing of superficial) standard. As one Hollywood actress is reported to have said recently: "We've become obsessed with beauty and the fountain of youth. . . . I'm really saddened by the way women mutilate [themselves] in search of that. I see women [including young women] . . . pulling this up and tucking that back. It's like a slippery slope. [You can't get off of it.] . . . It's really insane . . . what society is doing to women."[7]

In terms of preoccupation with self and a fixation on the physical, this is more than social insanity; it is spiritually destructive, and it accounts for much of the unhappiness women, including young women, face in the modern world. And if adults are preoccupied with appearance—tucking and nipping and implanting and remodeling everything that can be remodeled—those pressures and anxieties will certainly seep through to children. At some point the problem becomes what the Book of Mormon calls "vain imaginations" (1 Nephi 12:18). And in secular society both vanity *and* imagination run wild. One would truly need a great and spacious makeup kit to compete with beauty as portrayed in media all around us. Yet at the end of the day there would still be those "in the attitude of mocking and pointing their fingers" as Lehi saw (1 Nephi 8:27)[8] because however much one tries in the world of glamour and fashion, it will never be glamorous

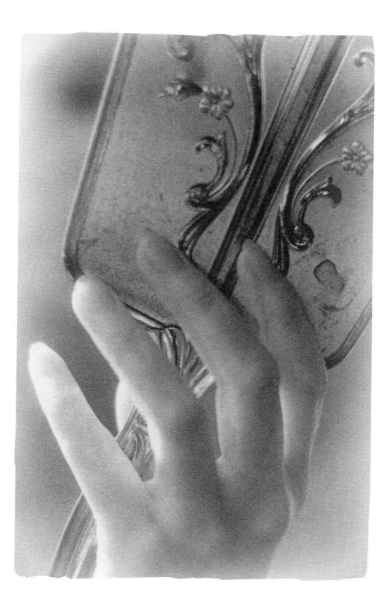

EVERY YOUNG WOMAN IS A

CHILD OF DESTINY AND

EVERY ADULT WOMAN A

POWERFUL FORCE FOR GOOD.

enough. A woman not of our faith once wrote something to the effect that in her years of working with beautiful women she had seen several things they all had in common, and not one of them had anything to do with sizes and shapes. She said the loveliest women she had known had a glow of health, a warm personality, a love of learning, stability of character, and integrity. If we may add the sweet and gentle Spirit of the Lord carried by such a woman, then this describes the loveliness of women in any age or time, *every* element of which is emphasized in and attainable through the blessings of the gospel of Jesus Christ.

Much has been said lately in entertainment media about the current craze for "reality shows." I am not sure what those are, but from the bottom of my heart I share this gospel reality with the beautiful generation of young women growing up in this Church.

My solemn declaration to you is that the Father and the Son did *in very fact* appear to the Prophet Joseph Smith, that he spoke the truth when he said, "In the midst of that light I saw two Personages, and they did *in reality* speak to me" (Joseph Smith—History 1:25; emphasis added). I testify that these divine beings did speak to him, that he heard Their eternal voices, and he saw Their glorified bodies (see Joseph Smith—History 1:24–25). That experience was as real in its own setting as the Apostle Thomas's was when the Savior said to him, "Reach hither thy finger, and behold my hands; and reach hither thy hand, and thrust it into my side: . . . be not faithless, but [be] believing" (John 20:27).

To my granddaughter and to every other young person in this Church I bear my personal witness that God is *in reality* our Father and Jesus Christ is *in reality* His Only Begotten Son in the flesh, the Savior and Redeemer of the world. I testify that this *really* is the Church and kingdom of God on earth, that true prophets have led this people in the past and a true prophet, President Gordon B. Hinckley, leads it now. May you know the unending love the leaders of the Church have for you and may you let the eternal realities of the gospel of Jesus Christ lift you above temporal concerns and teenage anxieties.

Notes

1. See "The Family: A Proclamation to the World," *Ensign,* November 1995, 102.

2. James E. Talmage, "The Eternity of Sex," *Young Woman's Journal,* October 1914, 602.

3. See J. Reuben Clark, in Conference Report, April 1940, 21, for a lengthy tribute to women of the Church.

4. Joseph Smith, *History of the Church of Jesus Christ of Latter-day Saints,* ed. B. H. Roberts, 2d ed. rev., 7 vols. (Salt Lake City: The Church of Jesus Christ of Latter-day Saints, 1932-51), 4:605.

5. *For the Strength of Youth* (Salt Lake City: The Church of Jesus Christ of Latter-day Saints, 2001), 15.

6. Julia DeVillers, *Teen People,* September 2005, 104.

7. Halle Berry, quoted in "Halle Slams 'Insane' Plastic Surgery," *This Is London,* August 2, 2004.

8. See Douglas Bassett, "Faces of Worldly Pride in the Book of Mormon," *Ensign,* October 2000, 51, for an excellent discussion of this issue.

THE SANCTITY
OF THE BODY

Susan W. Tanner

I recently returned from a visit where I welcomed into the world our newest little granddaughter, Elizabeth Claire Sandberg. She is perfect! I was awestruck, as I am each time a baby is born, with her fingers, toes, hair, beating heart, and her distinctive family characteristics—nose, chin, dimples. Her older brothers and sister were equally excited and fascinated by their tiny, perfect little sister. They seemed to sense a holiness in their home from the presence of a celestial spirit newly united with a pure physical body.

In the premortal realm we learned that the body was part of God's great plan of happiness for us. As it states in the family proclamation: "Spirit sons and daughters knew and worshiped God as their Eternal Father and accepted His plan by which His children could obtain a physical body and gain earthly experience to progress toward perfection and ultimately realize his or her divine destiny as an heir of eternal life."[1] In fact, we "shouted for joy" (Job 38:7) to be part of this plan.

Why were we so excited? We understood eternal truths about our bodies. We knew that our bodies would be in the image of God. We knew that our bodies would house our spirits. We also understood that our bodies would be subject to pain, illness, disabilities, and temptation. But we were willing, even eager, to accept these challenges because we knew that only with spirit and element inseparably connected could we progress to become like our Heavenly Father (see D&C 130:22) and "receive a fulness of joy" (D&C 93:33).

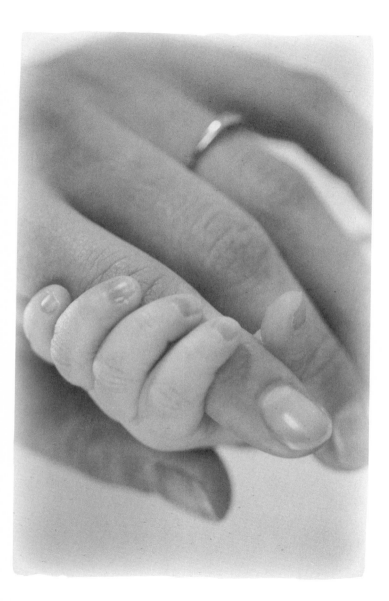

With the fulness of the gospel on the earth, we are again privileged to know these truths about the body. Joseph Smith taught: "We came to this earth that we might have a body and present it pure before God in the Celestial Kingdom. The great principle of happiness consists in having a body. The Devil has no body, and herein is his punishment."[2]

Satan learned these same eternal truths about the body, and yet his punishment is that he does not have one. Therefore he tries to do everything he can to get us to abuse or misuse this precious gift. He has filled the world with lies and deceptions about the body. He tempts many to defile this great gift of the body through unchastity, immodesty, self-indulgence, and addictions. He seduces some to despise their bodies; others he tempts to worship their bodies. In either case, he entices the world to regard the body merely as an object. In the face of so many satanic falsehoods about the body, I want to raise my voice today in support of the sanctity of the body. I testify that the body is a gift to be treated with gratitude and respect.

The scriptures declare that the body is a temple. It was Jesus Himself who first compared His body to a temple (see John 2:21). Later Paul admonished the people of Corinth, a wicked city teeming with all manner of lasciviousness and indecency: "Know ye not that ye are the temple of God, and that the Spirit of God dwelleth in you? If any man defile the temple of God, him shall God destroy; for the temple of God is holy, which temple ye are" (1 Corinthians 3:16–17).

What would happen if we truly treated our bodies as temples? The result would be a dramatic increase in chastity, modesty, observance of the Word of Wisdom, and a similar decrease in the problems of pornography and abuse, for we would regard the body, like the temple, as a sacred sanctuary of the

Spirit. Just as no unclean thing may enter the temple, we would be vigilant to keep impurity of any sort from entering the temple of our bodies.

Likewise, we would keep the outside of our bodily temples looking clean and beautiful to reflect the sacred and holy nature of what is inside, just as the Church does with its temples. We should dress and act in ways that reflect the sacred spirit inside us.

A short while ago as I visited one of the great tourist-filled cities of the world, I felt an overwhelming sadness that so many people in the world had fallen prey to Satan's deception that our bodies are merely objects to be flaunted and displayed openly. Imagine the contrast and my joy when I entered a classroom of modestly and appropriately dressed young women whose countenances glowed with goodness. I thought, *Here are eight beautiful girls who know how to show respect for their bodies and who know why they are doing it.* In *For the Strength of Youth* it says:

I TESTIFY THAT THE BODY IS

A GIFT TO BE TREATED WITH

GRATITUDE AND RESPECT.

"Your body is God's sacred creation. Respect it as a gift from God, and do not defile it in any way. Through your dress and appearance, you can show the Lord that you know how precious your body is. . . . The way you dress is a reflection of what you are on the inside."[3]

Modesty is more than a matter of avoiding revealing attire. It describes not only the altitude of hemlines and necklines but the attitude of our hearts. The word *modesty* means "measured." It is related to *moderate*. It implies "decency, and propriety . . . in thought, language, dress, and behavior."[4]

Moderation and appropriateness should govern all of our physical desires. A loving Heavenly Father has given us physical beauties and pleasures "both to please the eye and to gladden the heart" (D&C 59:18), but with this caution: that they are "made to be used, with judgment, not to excess, neither by extortion" (D&C 59:20). My husband used this

scripture to teach our children about the law of chastity. He said that the "word *extortion* . . . literally means to 'twist out [or against].' Our use of . . . the body must not be twisted [against] the divinely ordained purposes for which [it was] given. Physical pleasure is good in its proper time and place, but even then it must not become our god."[5]

The pleasures of the body can become an obsession for some; so too can the attention we give to our outward appearance. Sometimes there is a selfish excess of exercising, dieting, makeovers, and spending money on the latest fashions (see Alma 1:27).

I am troubled by the practice of extreme makeovers. Happiness comes from accepting the bodies we have been given as divine gifts and enhancing our natural attributes, not from remaking our bodies after the image of the world. The Lord wants us to be made over—but in His image,

43

HAPPINESS COMES FROM

ACCEPTING THE BODIES WE HAVE

BEEN GIVEN AS DIVINE GIFTS AND

ENHANCING OUR NATURAL

ATTRIBUTES, NOT FROM

REMAKING OUR BODIES.

not in the image of the world, by receiving His image in our countenances (see Alma 5:14, 19).

I remember well the insecurities I felt as a teenager with a bad case of acne. I tried to care for my skin properly. My parents helped me get medical attention. For years I even went without eating chocolate and all the greasy fast foods around which teens often socialize, but with no obvious healing consequences. It was difficult for me at that time to fully appreciate this body, which was giving me so much grief. But my good mother taught me a higher law. Over and over she said to me, "You must do everything you can to make your appearance pleasing, but the minute you walk out the door, forget yourself and start concentrating on others."

There it was. She was teaching me the Christlike principle of selflessness. Charity, or the pure love of Christ, "envieth not, and is not puffed up, seeketh not her own" (Moroni 7:45). When we become other-oriented, or selfless, we develop an inner beauty of spirit that glows in our outward appearance. This is how we make ourselves in the Lord's image rather than the world's and receive His image in our countenances. President Hinckley spoke of this very kind of beauty that comes as we learn to respect body, mind, and spirit. He said:

"Of all the creations of the Almighty, there is none more beautiful, none more inspiring than a lovely daughter of God who walks in virtue with an understanding of why she should do so, who honors and respects her body as a thing sacred and divine, who cultivates her mind and constantly enlarges the horizon of her understanding, who nurtures her spirit with everlasting truth."[6]

Oh, how I pray that all men and women will seek the beauty praised by the prophet—beauty of body, mind, and spirit!

The restored gospel teaches that there is an

intimate link between body, mind, and spirit. In the Word of Wisdom, for example, the spiritual and physical are intertwined. When we follow the Lord's law of health for our bodies, we are also promised wisdom to our spirits and knowledge to our minds (see D&C 89:19–21). The spiritual and physical truly are linked.

I remember an incident in my home growing up when my mother's sensitive spirit was affected by a physical indulgence. She had experimented with a new sweet roll recipe. They were big and rich and yummy—and very filling. Even my teenage brothers couldn't eat more than one. That night at family prayer my father called upon Mom to pray. She buried her head and didn't respond. He gently prodded her, "Is something wrong?" Finally she said, "I don't feel very spiritual tonight. I just ate three of those rich sweet rolls." I suppose that many of us have similarly offended our spirits at times by

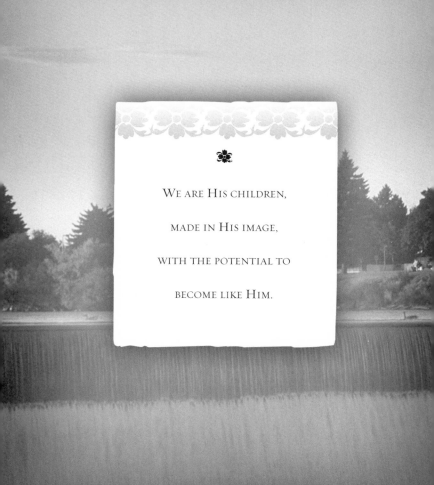

WE ARE HIS CHILDREN,

MADE IN HIS IMAGE,

WITH THE POTENTIAL TO

BECOME LIKE HIM.

physical indulgences. Especially substances forbidden in the Word of Wisdom have a harmful effect on our bodies and a numbing influence on our spiritual sensitivities. None of us can ignore this connection of our spirits and bodies.

These sacred bodies, for which we are so grateful, suffer from natural limitations. Some people are born with disabilities, and some suffer the pains of disease throughout their lives. All of us as we age experience our bodies gradually beginning to fail. When this happens, we long for the day when our bodies will be healed and whole. We look forward to the Resurrection that Jesus Christ made possible, when "the soul shall be restored to the body, and the body to the soul; yea, and every limb and joint shall be restored to its body; yea, even a hair of the head shall not be lost; but all things shall be restored to their proper and perfect frame" (Alma 40:23). I know that through Christ we can experience a fulness of joy that is available only when spirit and element are inseparably connected (see D&C 93:33).

Our bodies are our temples. We are not less but *more* like Heavenly Father because we are embodied. I testify that we are His children, made in His image, with the potential to become like Him. Let us treat this divine gift of the body with great care. Someday, if we are worthy, we shall receive a perfected, glorious body—pure and clean like my new little granddaughter, only inseparably bound to the spirit. And we shall shout for joy (see Job 38:7) to receive this gift again for which we have longed (see D&C 138:50). May we respect the sanctity of the body during mortality so that the Lord may sanctify and exalt it for eternity.

NOTES

1. "The Family: A Proclamation to the World," *Ensign*, November 1995, 102.

2. Joseph Smith, *The Words of Joseph Smith,* ed. Andrew F. Ehat and Lyndon W. Cook (Salt Lake City: Deseret Book Co., 1980), 60.

3. *For the Strength of Youth* (Salt Lake City: The Church of Jesus Christ of Latter-day Saints, 2001), 14–15.

4. In Daniel H. Ludlow, ed., *Encyclopedia of Mormonism,* 5 vols. (New York: Macmillan, 1992), 2:932.

5. John S. Tanner, "The Body As a Blessing," *Ensign,* July 1993, 10.

6. Gordon B. Hinckley, "Our Responsibility to Our Young Women," *Ensign,* September 1988, 11.

About the Authors

Elder Jeffrey R. Holland was ordained a member of the Quorum of the Twelve Apostles of The Church of Jesus Christ of Latter-day Saints on 23 June 1994. He had previously served as the ninth president of Brigham Young University, the Church commissioner of education, and dean of the College of Religious Education at BYU.

He received degrees in English and religious education from Brigham Young University. He obtained master and doctor of philosophy degrees in American Studies from Yale University. He is the author of six books.